EXTRAORD

52 *Lessons*
INCREASING YOUR LQ
(Living Quotient)

Copyright
2nd edition 2015
Marta Varee Pearson

ISBN: 0-9707456-7-5

This book may be ordered from Calla Publish.
Quantity discounts are available.
Contact us at:
action@trainingwithmarta.com
or
martaUUspeaker@gmail.com

Calla
Publish

1

DEDICATION

To my daughter, Nancee and your children,
Isaiah & Aden
Nancee, not of my womb, Truly of my soul.
You have helped to make my life extraordinary.
I know that you will continue to do the same for
Isaiah and Aden as they will do for you.
I hope the lessons that I have provided to you
we both will pass on to your sons.

To my son Scott,
who struggled along with me
while I learned what esteem really is.
You are a wonderful father,
a caring brother to your sister,
A loving husband
and an attentive son to me.
You make me proud.

Because of you both,
my heart swells with pride.

To Pam,
My sister not of birth, friend & guide.
I am always thankful that you entered my life.

And finally,
to Sherley, Alyce, Deanna & especially Dante
as well as all the friends, associates and clients
who provided feedback and encouragement,
thank you.

EXTRAORDINARY LIVING
in
52 LESSONS
INCREASING YOUR LQ
(Living Quotient)

Helping People
"Put the Puzzle Pieces in Place"

You already have all the pieces.
We'll guide you in
putting them in place.

02/28/16

*May we have
a long and fun filled
friendship.
In fellowship
& love,
Marta*

INTRODUCTION

Children come into the world
with everything they need.
They arrive with an intrinsic value
and infinite ability to:
love, do, feel, explore, learn & know.

Many people are familiar with the terms
IQ (Intelligence Quotient
& EQ (Emotional Quotient).

IQ, representing our level of intellectual capacity,
is an indicator of ability to learn, understand,
reason or to deal with new or trying situations.
It is not always reflective of the reality.
There are many with high IQs
who function poorly.

EQ, a relatively new concept,
represents ability to experience emotion.
Many fail to exercise this ability properly.

IQ & EQ represent possibilities
and are passive.

LQ is active.
LQ is one's Living Quotient.
LQ is the
active experience of Living Extraordinarily.

Measuring a child's LQ is as simple as
watching them experience any day.

How many days must be viewed
before an adult's LQ
can even begin to be measured.
Existing,
as most adults do,
is not enough.
Extraordinary Living is the answer.

This book will help you
to reacquaint yourself with the elements that
comprise a healthy Living Quotient.

Only you can apply it to increase your own
Living Quotient.

HOW TO USE THIS BOOK

As a therapist, teacher, coach,
parent, grandparent and friend
I have often been asked
"How much time will it take to...
Learn
Heal
Grow
Change?

My reply to each inquiry is always the same.

It is not how long or how much time it takes.
Rather it is what you do with the time that matters.

When asked "when will I know or understand?"
My reply is that DOING is more important
than knowing and understanding.
All of the knowledge and understanding in the
world will not make your life different.
Change will not occur until you ACTIVELY DO.

This book is to provide a course for your DOING.

ACTION 1
Read the book and think about which chapters you
will work on to make your living extraordinary.

ACTION 2
Go back to those chapters & develop habits that will
make the definitions, concepts, strategies & skills
an active part of daily living.

ACTION 3
Take your time. Living is the journey
not the arrival at a destination.
Savor a chapter a week. Develop the habits.

ACTION 4
Commit yourself to living each day Extraordinarily.
Return to the healthy roots of organic childhood
when _everything_ was extraordinary.

ACTION 5
Live as an Active, not a passive.
Move past existence to
EXTRAORDINARY LIVING.

GUIDE

A short guide to growth

Congratulations!

You've decided to become proactive in your life.

Good for you.

Look for...

 DEFINITIONS

 ACTION STEPS

 REFLECTIONS

Time to start!

 **REMEMBER TO ALWAYS START WITH A DEFINITION**

EXTRAORDINARY LIVING in 52 LESSONS

ABOUT THE AUTHOR

Marta Varee Pearson, President of Training With Marta, is a sought after speaker, trainer, coach & consultant. Her background includes a private practice spanning 14 years as a sexual abuse recovery therapist. Her interest stems from her own history of abuse & the non-availability of appropriate treatment options during her recovery.

Personally, Marta overcame a childhood of adversity which included sexual abuse by relatives from the age of 3 to 17. Three suicide attempts, the first at 15, resulted in her search for a way to live and the development of the Unicorn Philosophy of Extraordinary Living Principles™ that provided the way ultimately resulting in the Animate Therapeutic Process™,the ATP™ Group Individual Formats.

She earned a bachelor degree in Human Behavior at the University of Kentucky & a Master of Science Degree in Law Enforcement/ Juvenile Justice Administration from Eastern KY Univ. She amassed more than 300 hours of training in Trauma & Abuse issues.

She has taught at Hyde Boarding School, elementary through high school for public school systems in Topsham and Brunswick Maine, and Hillsborough County FL, Andover College in Portland & for the University of Maine at Augusta at its main campus in Augusta and campuses in Brunswick and at Lewiston Auburn College. Most recently she taught at Springfield College in Tampa Florida.

Marta has been much in demand as a trainer with professionals in the fields of sexual abuse recovery through public workshops for therapists and other helping professionals including teachers and education facility staffs.

She provided training to the staff at the Augusta Mental Health Institute on "Advanced Treatment of the Adult Violated As Child Sexually" over a four-year period. She developed the first for credit class for the University of Maine on sexual abuse treatment and continued to teach that well received class for them for 8 years.

For 6 years Marta trained State of Maine Foster Parents in "Parenting Sexually Abused Children", "Self-Esteem Recognition", "Effective Communication Skills", "Developing Trusting Relationships" & other topics.

Marta made numerous television appearances including 3 on the

Increasing your IQ (Living Quotient)

Sally Jessy Raphael Show, 2 on Geraldo and 1 on Donahue as well as local television programs.

She has added author to her list of accomplishments. Besides this one her books include *"Living - an Extraordinary Banquet"*, *"Extraordinary Living in 52 Lessons"*, *"Esteem Recognition: Our Core & Foundation"*, *"Trust & Effective Communication"*, *"Stress is a Marble - Spin It Your Way"*, and *"Growth Strategies for Effective Living"*.

Each of her books is available for presentation in several formats, as a keynote speech, seminar or workshop. Others available include "Regaining Civility in an Angry World", "Life Sucks, So Why Aren't You Reaching for a Straw?!" overcoming adversity, "From victim to Living - the stages beyond surviving" trauma recovery and "'I' precedes 'T' in the Alphabet, Affirming Life for Team Building".

In addition to her therapeutic work, Marta brings a wide range of practical experience to her presentations. She worked 8 years as a civil rights investigator and administrator and 30 years as a trainer. She has worked also as a postal clerk, nurse aide, restaurant and cocktail waitress, store and private detective, reading tutor, census worker, inventory clerk, call center advisor, probation & parole classification/treatment officer and as a Foster Parent Recruiter-Licensor-Supervisor for a therapeutic mental health program.

She presents sermons and workshop at Unitarian Universalist churches and for other denominations.

Marta is a birth parent, adoptive parent, stepparent, grand and great-grandparent and former foster parent. She grew up in northern Indiana, lived a temporary 16 years in Kentucky and for 24 years resided in Maine. Marta believes that her move to Maine corrected the mistake that the stork made when it overshot her birth drop off point. She lived 6 years in Washington state. When she tired of winter she determined to make Florida her home. She now resides permanently in Tampa Florida

Marta is available to provide service in your area.
Choose from a speech, workshop, class, coaching or consultation.
You may contact her at:
Training with Marta Tampa FL 813-495-3021
action@trainingwithmarta.com or
martaUUspeaker@gmail.com
View her websites: trainingwithmarta.com & martaUUspeaker.com

TABLE OF CONTENTS

TABLE OF CONTENTS

1ST SEASON

LESSON 1 - DEFINITIONS, SOCIETY & ORGANICS

For a moment, we are going to discuss the color green?

Have you assumed that we are
thinking about the same green?

There is
true green,
bright green,
sea green,
lime green & more.

> ➤DEFINITION A roadmap or blueprint that allows us to function together in a healthy, efficient & productive manner.

Definitions
are what allow us to talk about
the same thing at the same time.

Whenever and whatever one does
it must start with a definition.
Each subject we explore will start
with a definition that we will use.
It may not be a traditional definition society is using.
It may, in fact, be a definition that is a
total contradiction to the societal status quo.
While it may be a contradiction in that way,
It may also be a confirmation of something that
you have felt deep inside without -
the ability to express it yourself.
Interesting, huh?

14

➤SOCIETY
People who share like ideas, interests, motivations & goals who value, respect, honor support & help each other.

The purpose of society is to maintain
the health and well-being
of the individuals who comprise it.

Too often society's purpose is to
maintain its own status quo
to the detriment of
the individual and
ultimately society itself.

**Are
we
society
or
is
society
us?**

It is our responsibility to define & shape society.
We either do it or we abdicate our right to complain.

ORGANICS

> **ORGANIC CHILD**
> A
> **healthy
> child,
> uncontaminated
> by
> adults,
> usually
> nonexistent
> past
> the
> age
> of
> 7.**

Did you ever
play the game
"telegraph?"
A message is repeated
by one person to another
to the end of the line.
The resulting
message
doesn't resemble the
original.

What you
needed to
know came
into the
world with
you.

The messages of
living
passed down thru
the
generations
have degraded
and become
distorted.

➤ORGANIC ADULT
**One who nurtures one's self.
As a parent - one who nurtures her/his
charges & teaches them how to be healthy,
independent, thinking, functioning
individuals.**

Children experience & learn

from the benefit of play.
Adults disdain it.

Children find wonder in
all of the world's gifts.

Adults can
relearn a
valuable
lesson from
childhood.

**Consider,
children
don't
experience
shame
or
embarrassment
until
we
teach
them
how
to.**

17

LESSON 2 - BUBBLE BLOWERS, LEVELS & ELEVATORS

**It's all about you.
It's never about anyone else.
When you make a change your life is
different even when no one else changes.**

Make a toy bubble blower
with your hand.

Your thumb is pointed at the universe
One finger at the person you want to change.

Three fingers are pointed at you.
You must change 3 times over before

you can expect change from anyone else.
Even if they don't change, your live is different.

LEVELS

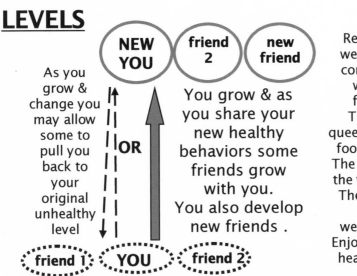

Remember,
we are most
comfortable
with the
familiar.
The prom
queen dates the
football hero.
The nerd dates
the wallflower.
There will be
loss as
well as gain.
Enjoy your new
healthy level.

18

When you press the down button in an elevator

you go **down**

When you press the up you go **UP**

The elevator has no choice except to go where the button indicates it is to go.

No matter which of your buttons another person pushes, you choose the direction you will go.

No one MAKES you angry. You take whatever they say and choose the emotion you experience. Only you make you happy, sad, glad or mad.

You are not an elevator.

No matter what buttons other people push you always have the ability to choose the direction you will go.

LESSON 3 - ESTEEM: THE BEGINNING
esteem, the infant

When you walk into a room and see an infant, don't you smile and feel good just because it's there?

Is it because you know they'll be a math expert one day,
or an
important executive?

Of course not!
At that point you have
no idea what they will be.
You only have your
hopes and dreams
for them.

You love them
and feel good
in their presence
just because
they
exist.

esteem, the transition

Prior to the age of 7 when children are in preschool & kindergarten, every effort is rewarded. The child is valued.

Beginning around the age of 7, at the time students enter 2nd grade, the judging begins.

The child who tries his best and earns a C grade feels lower esteem than the one who earns an A.

The child who's not as popular as the rest feels lower esteem.

The adult who loses her job through layoff beyond her control and the man who has difficulty maintaining relationships - each experiences low esteem.

Society traditionally defines esteem as accomplishment and ability.

BEFORE GOING FURTHER - HOW DO YOU DEFINE ESTEEM?

CHAPTER 4 - ESTEEM: REDEFINED

Remember the feelings we have for the infant.

Esteem must be based on things that you can control.

Your value is in your existence
not in how much or how well you do.

There is no need to work on your value.

>ESTEEM

SPECIALNESS
DUE
to
EXISTENCE

You can
and will
work
on how much
you do
&
how well
you do
things.

Self-confidence

Society has mistakenly taught us that
we can build our self-esteem.

CAUTION!
What can be
built
can be torn
down

What we build
through practice and improvement
is
SELF-CONFIDENCE

**Special
IS
who you
are
NOT
what you
do.**

➤**SELF CONFIDENCE**
WHAT WE DO

SELF-ESTEEM
Is who we are.

CHAPTER 5 - ESTEEM: RECOGNITION

It is not that your esteem rises and falls with
circumstances that come into your life,
your esteem is constant.
The problem is
a failure to recognize
what is already and always present.

You are not
a ghost.
Do not let your value
materialize
and
dematerialize
based on
circumstances.

Get off the
roller coaster
that
circumstances
outside
of your control
puts you on.

It is important enough to repeat:
SELF-ESTEEM is who you are,
not what you do.
Recognize that it is always present.

Never have 'a bad hair' day.

Your
hair, appearance, job, income,
relationship status
and other such criteria
do not determine your
self-esteem

Practice creates greater
self-confidence
(what you do)

and
the more you do the greater
your self-confidence.

YOU
have
CHOICE
in how
you
RESPOND
to circumstance.
That is
self-confidence.

Esteem
(value)
is
always
present.

Recognize
it.

✳✳

Need to build your
esteem recognition?

Take
3x5
index cards

Write

I am special
because I exist!

Post by your bed,
sock drawer,
bathroom mirror,
in the kitchen & car.

Read no less than 3
times a day until you
recognize its reality!

EXTRAORDINARY LIVING in 52 LESSONS
cards info on page 126.

LESSON 6 - SELFNESS

>**SELFISHNESS**
an
artificial
ranking
system
appropriate
in
nonpersonal
situations.

In a classroom of children everyone can't line up at the same time. The alphabet is used as an artificial ranking system. 'A' has more right and privilege to line up than the rest of the alphabet. Then 'B' has the right, then 'C'...

On the job every employee can't have the same vacation period. Seniority is used as a ranking system.

In a personal situation-
When someone asks for your time or piece of the pie after they have already had their share, they are asking you to rank your needs as less important than theirs. They are asking you to be 'selfless'.

Have you ever flown?
When emergency
procedures are explained
you are informed that if the
oxygen masks drop down you
are to put yours on 1st & if
traveling with a child
put the child's on 2nd.

You can't help anyone else
if you are struggling.

➤SELFNESS
recognizing
one's
own
need
and
fulfilling
it
without
direct
harm
to
another.

It is your
responsibility
to fill your needs.
It is not your
responsibility
to fill another's
nor theirs
to fill yours.

When you give up
what you need,
when you base your decision
on the needs of another-
resentment often follows.

You will take back,
in some form,
what you gave.
You will snap at them
over a minor matter
or
become angry totally out of
proportion to the incident.

Because there is nothing free in this world.

LESSON 7 - ACTION VS. KNOWLEDGE

> **KNOWLEDGE**
> **understanding**

Knowledge/Understanding is not necessary for an action to be successful.

Throw a rock into a pond and what do you get?
Triangular or Square ripples?
Circular ripples?!

Knowledge and Understanding may prevent you from doing the very thing you want to do.

We don't have to have knowledge
or
understand
the physics involved to get the result.

ACTION precedes knowledge.

**ACTION is required to acquire knowledge.
You must:
ask, read,
listen or watch
-
all are actions.**

**✳✶✶
Stop waiting for knowledge/understanding.
That may lead to paralysis.**

28

What one knows
changes
nothing.
What one does
can change
everything.

> **➤ACTION**
> **the**
> **doing**
> **that**
> **creates**
> **change**
> **and**
> **may**
> **lead**
> **to**
> **learning**
> **or**
> **understanding;**
> **what one does.**

Not knowing
why you love
doesn't stop
you from
loving.

Even a step back is not
a backward step
when it gets you
where you want to go.

**Take a step,
evaluate your new understanding or
knowledge and plan your next step.**

LESSON 8 -
PERSONAL RESPONSIBILITY vs.
GUILT

➤**GUILT**

a Self

Imposed

Non-reality

＊Self Imposed
No one else
makes you
feel badly,
you take what
they say and
make it so.

＊Non-reality
You take the event
and turn it around
180 degrees to allow
yourself to feel badly.

No one ever
died from
guilt.
So
if you want it,
keep it.

No one
can stop
you from
feeling
guilty
except
you.

Guilt
is a
non-productive
artificially
created
emotion.

Guilt just allows you to feel bad
and keeps you stuck.

➤ PERSONAL RESPONSIBILITY
Taking action to achieve a purpose.
The condition opposite to guilt.

GUILT
It's awful that I'm
not spending
enough time with
my daughter.

Responsibility
moves
you
to
where
you
want
to
be.

RESPONSIBILITY

"I'm not spending enough
time with my daughter.

I'm going to have lunch
with her in the school cafe-
teria at least twice a month
and
be her scout troop leader
so we spend time together".

When you want to rid yourself of GUILT,
REDEFINE IT
&
take the necessary
action.

LESSON 9 - GUIDELINE, RULES & ACCOUNTABILITY

> **➤RULES A set of laws;**
> **regulation for standard procedure.**

	Situation: Rule = **No food in the family room.**
Too few	Someone leaves unfinished soda in the room.
Then too many	New rule created.
	Another new rule when someone leaves candy wrappers.
May become contradictory Rigid	Person who is sick needs to drink ginger ale. Result: No exceptions or rules broken.
Uneven enforcement	One parent enforces the rule & the other one lets it slide.
Applies to the ones who don't follow procedures & to those who do as well	Even applies to people who clean up after themselves. People who clean up after themselves are penalized by the rule they don't need.
Outwardly enforced by rules police	People who don't follow the rule are not self accountable and are policed by others.

➤**GUIDELINE**
**Self-enforcing
principle
for
determining
a
course
of
action.**

One question fits all
circumstances:

Is it
Safe
and does it
Show Respect
for
**Self
Others
&
Property**?

In the no food in the family room situation -

A guideline is applied because there is a
problem with persons not being responsible
for the mess that they create.

It has nothing to do with the food.

Therefore:
People who clean up eat in the room.
People who leave a mess don't eat there
until they become responsible & clean up.

They no longer hold everyone else hostage
to their lack of responsible actions
as they do with a set of rules.

➤**ACCOUNTABILITY**
Being responsible for ones actions.

LESSON 10 - BOUNDARIES & LIMITS

> **Human Boundaries** are flexible, self-imposed, announced, and self-guarded.

Boundaries between cities, states & countries are rigid and unmovable.

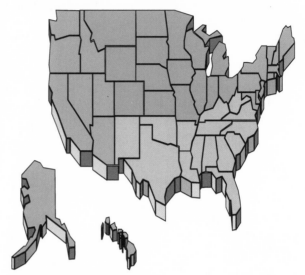

Human boundaries
must be
flexible
and depend on the current needs of the individual.

When one is well,
boundaries are close in to allow the closeness of others.
When one is sick,
boundaries are farther out
to allow space for healing.

It is
your
responsibility to
**set your
boundaries**
and to
not allow
others to
set them for you.

It is your responsibility to
**announce
your boundaries**
so that others
know what you expect.

It is your responsibility to
guard your boundaries
& to keep people at the distance you want them.
Don't blame them when you open the gate & let them in.

➤LIMITS
Selecting what one will share, with whom and when.

You have
the right & the responsibility
to choose
what you talk about,
who you will talk with,
and when you will talk.

✳✳CHOOSE

LESSON 11 - CONTROLS, POWER & HABIT

> ➤CONTROL
> **Exercise of or lack of exercise of power and ability to effect change.**

There are two types of control.

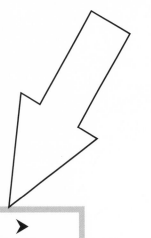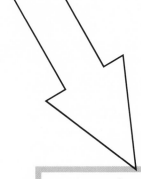

➤
INTERNAL CONTROL
An absolute power & ability to effect change.

➤
EXTERNAL CONTROL
An absolute lack of power and ability to effect change no matter how hard one tries or what one does.

You plan to have a picnic.

EXTERNAL CONTROL

Issuing invitations
based on who will or won't
accepts the invitation
or
who will or won't get along.
You have no control over
those things.

A guest calls & asks if she
should bring a dessert.
You tell her yes to avoid
hurting her feelings or
no, it's covered.

She brings a pie anyway.
You anguish over whether
or not she will be hurt
if you don't serve it.

Because it rains you wish you
had picked another day even
though it is impossible to pick
a day when it won't rain.

These are things you
CAN'T
Control.

➡

Look to what you can.

INTERNAL CONTROL

You control
the decision of
who to invite as guests
because you want
them to attend.

You plan the menu:
hotdogs, slaw
& watermelon.

Thank her and offer to
let her take it home.
When she says keep it -
put it aside for your
next day meal &
serve your
planned menu.

You can call people &:
cancel or
tell them to wear
swimsuits or
set up a tent.

**CONTROL WHAT IS
POSSIBLE.
Let go of what isn't!**

➤HABIT
**Repetitive acts
that lead to a usual
mode of action.**

➤POWER
**The ability to
effect change
through action.**

LESSON 12 - FAMILY vs. RELATIVES

> **RELATIVE**
> **Person who is accidentally related by birth, adoption or marriage. May or may not be family.**

Relatives are accidents.

You had no choice or control over who your relatives are.

You have no ability to change relatives into the kind of people you want them to be.

Letting go of unhealthy relatives may allow them to change & come back into your life later.

You can't reach for family as long as you cling to relatives. Don't gamble on them.

Families are created.

Family may be the brother that you can't imagine not having in your life.

Family may be the next door neighbor who shares your values and your interests and who treats you as family .

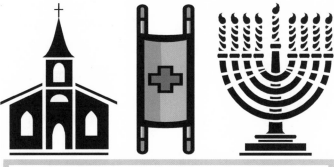

➤FAMILY Person who shares your values & interests & treats you with love, kindness, respect and honor. May or may not be relatives.

Family may be found at your job or in the organization you volunteer time to or your religious community.

You deserve family.

Create one.

LESSON 13 - THE LIVING WELL™

> ➤
> **The LIVING WELL™ The use of action as the prime factor in change, not time.**

Your life is a well filled by experiences.

Poison drops into your well with every disappointment, criticism, putdown, hurt, or failure whether inflicted from outside or from within.

1000 drops of poison

A poisoned well doesn't sustain life.

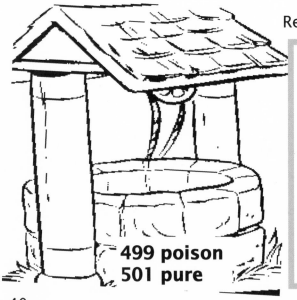

499 poison 501 pure

Replace the poison.

> ✳✳✳
> **Surround yourself with people who are positive and supportive.**

FILLING YOUR WELL

A LIFE (well)
filled with PURE (water)
is one nourished by
the things one enjoys
[reading, picnics, skiing,
movies, success]
&
by the people who
provide support
[family, friends, social &
professional associates]

**NEVER
accept negative
from others
or from yourself.**

Remember that
evaporation
is a law of nature
that applies to
water wells

as well as to your living well.

**1000
drops of
pure**

**Because
of
evaporation
filling
your
well
must
be
a
lifelong
pleasure.**

NOTES

2ND SEASON

LESSON 14 - BREATHING

> **➤BREATHING**
> to FULLY draw air into
> & expel from the lungs;
> a lost skill.

We can
do without
food
for
many days.

We can do without water for several days.

We can
do without
air
for only
seconds.

THE PROCESS

When you are afraid, confused, frustrated,
or concerned your breathing becomes
shallow or you hold your breath.

Suffocation is a primal fear.

Your
mind
registers
danger.

Your body reacts
by pumping
adrenaline
to give you
strength to fight
or run away,
as the cave dweller
ran away from the
saber tooth tiger.

The things you fear or that cause you concern can no
longer be physically fought or run away from.
Escape requires thought.

Adrenaline is not a thinking chemical. It stops the thinking process.

While taking a test you become afraid because you can't remember the answers to the next set of questions. You have begun to breath shallowly and adrenaline has started to flow.

BREATHE

To pass that test, put the pencil down and breathe. Everytime you feel concern, repeat.

You can't think if you don't have air!

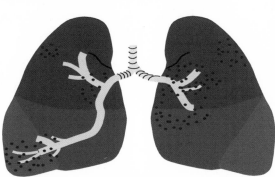

Take 3 complete, truly deep breaths and see how you feel... DIZZY?

Feel good?

Probably the first time your lungs have experienced real breathing in a long time.

You deserve that feeling all the time.

Practice breathing when you wake up, at noon, in the evening & at bedtime.

Your body will thank you.

LESSON 15 - OPTIONS THINKING & DECISION MAKING

> **OPTIONS**
> **Full range of possibilities**

No, this is not the test to determine whether you are an optimist (1/2 full) or a pessimist (1/2 empty)

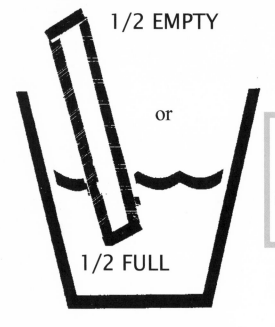

1/2 EMPTY

or

1/2 FULL

It's both. Don't eliminate options.

There is never a time when there are no options.

Never eliminate an option until all options have been explored

There is seldom a time when there is only one option.

There are times when there are no options one likes.

➤DECISION MAKING
**Ability to
discern all options,
select an option for action
& implement the action
in a timely manner.**

With enough practice,
can one learn to make the right
decision most of the time?

NO!

There is no
such thing as a
RIGHT decision
-
only decisions
with
positive or
negative
outcomes.

We are not
born with
decision
making
skill.
With practice
we learn
the skill.

**Our
capacity
to
decide
is
infinite!
We're
not
limited
to
3,948,322
decisions.**

With practice one will learn
to make decisions
that have
positive outcomes
most of the time.

LESSON 16 - SOLUTIONS & CHANGE

➤**SOLUTION**
**Course of action selected from all options
that does not create other
equal or greater problems.**

Solutions are created through ones ACTIONS.
LOOK at ALL options

SELECT an option.

ACT upon the option.

EVALUATE the outcome.

REPEAT process until the outcome is positive.

Positive Outcome = Solution

The solution may not be:
what one wants, ideal or easy;
or may be only a partial solution.

When an chosen action places us in a position
more positive than the one we began in
it is a solution.

> **CHANGE**
> **To make different.**

Did you eat today the same foods that you ate yesterday?

Will you wear the same clothes tomorrow
that you are wearing today?
Will you wear them for a third and forth day?

Change is not an enemy.

We must learn to embrace it as an ally.

C **CONSTANT** - It is a part of everyday living. Don't be caught off guard. Expect it.

H **HUMOR** - Look for it. Use it to get from the old to the new. Laughter keeps us sane.

A **ABILITY** - Without change there is no need to test or develop our abilities.

N **NECESSITY** - As winter is a necessity for growth in spring so change is for people.

G **GROWTH** - Riding a bike requires pedaling or one falls. Growing prevents falling.

E **EXCITEMENT & ENERGY** - Boredom is draining.
Change ➔ Excitement ➔ Energy

LESSON 17 - TENSION

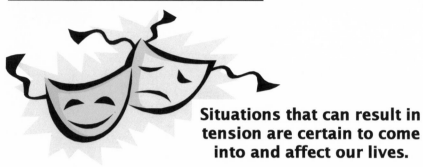

Situations that can result in tension are certain to come into and affect our lives.

> **➤TENSION**
> **events of living represented by both the positive and the negative; interests, excitement, enjoyment, pleasure; problems, disagreements, pain, inactivity.**

Consider life a tightrope.

Not enough tension, the rope sags. RESULT - you fall off.

Too much tension, the rope breaks. RESULT - you fall off.

Just the right amount of tension is necessary to walk that tightrope of life.

We also do it everyday at mealtime.

Too little spice, the meal is boring & unappetizing.

Too much spice, the meal is overwhelming and inedible.

The right amount = a great meal

TENSION WORKSHEETS

POSITIVE TENSIONS THAT MAY LEAD TO OVERFLOW

NEGATIVE TENSIONS THAT MAY LEAD TO OVERFLOW

LESSON 18 - STRESS IS A MARBLE™

Everyone knows
it wasn't the
pyramid
that broke the
camel's back.
It was the
last straw.

**View each tension (problem) as a marble.
Marbles are easy to spin out of the way.
Boulders are unmovable.**

When we don't act on the tensions
that come into our lives it, builds.

When tension builds to an overwhelming amount,
it becomes stress & we **spin out of control.**

OVERFLOW

What happens when you continue to drop marbles into a glass half filled with water?

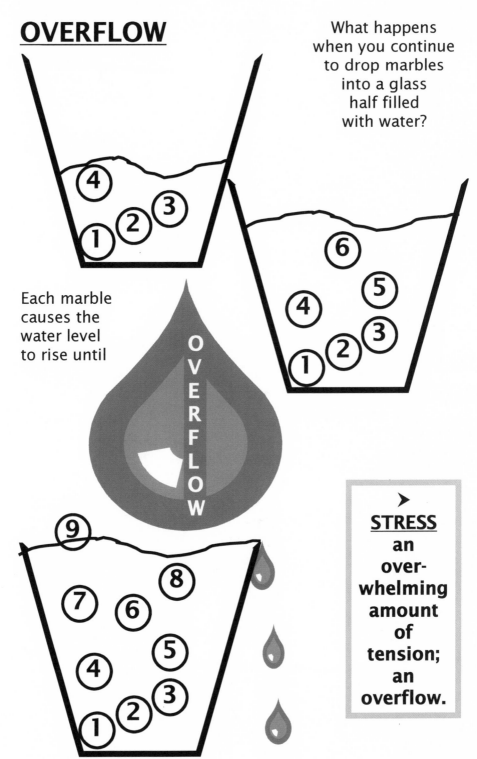

Each marble causes the water level to rise until

OVERFLOW

> STRESS an over-whelming amount of tension; an overflow.

LESSON 19 - SPIN IT (STRESS) YOUR WAY

Because it is the one too many tensions (marbles) causing overflow that creates the stress one must evaluate each tension as it enters one's life.

LOSE YOUR MARBLES

EVALUATE

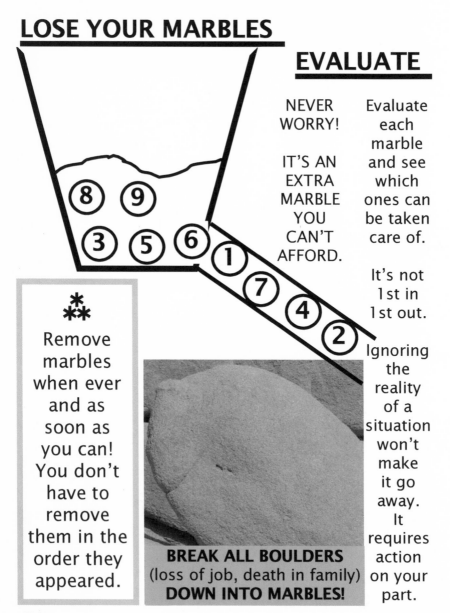

NEVER WORRY!

IT'S AN EXTRA MARBLE YOU CAN'T AFFORD.

Evaluate each marble and see which ones can be taken care of.

It's not 1st in 1st out.

Ignoring the reality of a situation won't make it go away. It requires action on your part.

✳
✳✳
Remove marbles when ever and as soon as you can! You don't have to remove them in the order they appeared.

BREAK ALL BOULDERS
(loss of job, death in family)
DOWN INTO MARBLES!

Some people can hold 4 marbles in their life
before they overflow.
Some can hold 7, some 10 and some only 2.
Know your limit and observe it.

THE NUMBER OF MARBLES IN MY LIFE BEFORE OVERFLOW	

FLOW SHEET

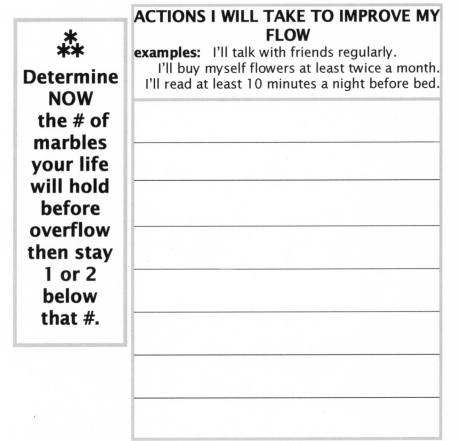

Determine NOW the # of marbles your life will hold before overflow then stay 1 or 2 below that #.

ACTIONS I WILL TAKE TO IMPROVE MY FLOW

examples: I'll talk with friends regularly.
I'll buy myself flowers at least twice a month.
I'll read at least 10 minutes a night before bed.

order your
Stress is a Marble paperweight
page 126.

LESSON 20 - FEAR

Before looking at the next page
fill in the blanks below.

My definition of fear is -

_____

_____

The words society uses to describe a person who
experiences fear are -

_____   _____

_____   _____

Now look below. Do any of yours match the ones listed?

Society teaches us to
view fear as
undesirable.

Is the definition
you wrote
negative?

When asked, most people define it as a loss of:
control, power or knowledge.
(unknown   uncontrollable   weakness)

Society doesn't provide a
positive definition or
positive words to describe
the event of
experiencing fear.

No wonder
we don't want
to be afraid.

Yellow Chicken Coward Yellow-belly Sissy

Fear is
not the
enemy.
It is a
safety
device.

A positive definition for fear allows
one to use fear for what it is:
a tool to keep one safe

> **FEAR**
**a reasonable response
to a real or perceived danger.**

real danger: A snowy day in winter.

reasonable response:
You drive more slowly & carefully than usual.

Recognizing,
accepting
&
acting on
fear
is a
daily
responsible
action
for
one's own
well-being.

perceived danger:
A sunny winter day two days
after a winter storm with
melting snow and ice.

reasonable response:
After the sun goes down and
It is again freezing you
perceive that because of
weather conditions ice could
have formed from the day's
melt and you drive more
slowly & carefully than usual.

Paranoia:
Believing there is ice on the
road on a sunny 4th of July.

LESSON 21 - ANGER

> **➤ANGER**
> **a**
> **flashfire**
> **response**
> **to an**
> **immediate**
> **situation**
> **when**
> **one**
> **experiences**
> **or may**
> **experience**
> **hurt or**
> **harm.**

Unpleasant, unexpected,
unfair and irritating events
fuel the
very real emotion of anger.

When you don't put logs on the fire
in the fireplace the fire dies.

True anger is short lived.
When anger isn't fed it dies.

While anger and fear may result from the same
situation, anger is seldom the primary emotion.

Because society teaches us to ignore fear,
when only fear or both fear & anger are present
we often skip over the fear
and only react with anger.

Your small child is riding a scooter in the yard.
Suddenly, he rolls toward the street.

You reach him just before he
rolls off the curb
into the street and into
the path of an oncoming car.

When you
reach the
child do you:
hug him &
tell him how
frightened
you were
for him?

Do you say how glad you are that he is safe?

Not likely. Most people would:
Grab him & shake him.
Yell.
Demand to know why he wasn't more careful.
Order him into the house.

Your fear has not been expressed as fear.

Even when you say how frightened you were
the tone of your voice and the look on your face resemble
anger more than fear.

And thus,
the child learns to express his fear as anger
as we did before him.

People today, children & adults, are not
so much angry as they are afraid.

BULLIES AREN'T ANGRY - THEY ARE AFRAID

LESSON 22 - PSEUDOANGER, ANXIETY, PANIC & RAGE

> ## ➤PSEUDOANGER
> ### fear masquerading as anger.

Because society doesn't teach one to address fear

one often skips right over fear

& reacts with false anger because one is not able to

recognize, accept, or express the fear.

One can't rid one self of anger that doesn't exist.

When anger won't go away, check for the underlying fear that may be present.

FEAR (1st level) **whispers**.

> ## ➤ANXIETY
> ### 2nd level of fear; the inner voice URGENTLY trying to get a message through.

ANXIETY speaks a bit louder & taps on the shoulder.

> ## ➤PANIC
> ### 3rd level of fear; the inner voice DESPERATELY trying to get a message through.

PANIC screams, grabs you & shakes you until someone comes to help.

➤RAGE
Illogical, counterproductive
(often destructive) response
resulting from fear, anger or pseudoanger
fueled by feelings of powerlessness or
personal insecurities.

Look at a person
who has a minor
car accident & is
afraid both of
being late and
the cost of repairs.

Unable or unwilling to
look at his fear he
responds in a rage &
hits the other driver.
Result = arrest & jail.

His illogical response is
Counterproductive and destructive.

HE IS NOW SURE TO BE LATE.
His repair costs are nothing compared to
BAIL MONEY & ATTORNEY FEES.

The damage to his reputation and a criminal record
add further to the
illogical nature of the response.

LESSON 23 -
TRUST: TESTING THE TRADITIONAL

trust, the traditional

Before going further,
write your own definition of trust.
Don't cheat yourself
by looking beyond this box!

_____

_____

_____

_____

_____

5 individuals were asked to
provide their definition of trust.

1. When someone tells me the truth.

2. When a person supports me.

3. People keep their promises.

4. When people don't hurt me.

5. When a friend doesn't betray my
   confidence when I tell them something.

DID YOURS MATCH ANY OF THE 5?
How many words the same?
How many different?

There are
5
basic problems
with traditional definitions
and
we will talk about them
after a quick & easy test.

trust, the test

DO A QUICK TEST.

Provide the word that comes to mind.

in/_____   salt/_____

yes/_____   left/_____

up/_____   positive/_____

Did you know the answers? Sure you did.

You knew the answers because
there is little in life that has no opposite.
Except when society looks at trust.
Society says trust is only a positive
without a negative other half.

LESSON 24 - TRUST: THE PROBLEMS

You were asked on the previous page to provide a definition for trust. Had you ever thought of what you looked for & how you experienced trust?

PROBLEM 1

Most people haven't & that's

PROBLEM 2 - TOO MANY WORDS.

When too many words are used it's hard to transfer definitions from one person to another.

PROBLEM 3

LACK OF MATCH

When one person's words don't exactly match those of another person it will be difficult, if not impossible, to experience trust together.

Each is looking for something different.

All of the definitions on page 62 & those that most people develop are external.

PROBLEM 4

trust in the other person takes power out of your hands.

When you trust,
it is **yourself** you trust to see the reality around you.
Trust is not in the other person.

PROBLEM 5

elimination of half the possibilities

Sugar is neither positive nor negative. It is neutral.
To a diabetic sugar has a negative application.
To a healthy person, a positive application.

So it is with trust. Trust is neutral and has
both positive and negative applications.

The world is made up of two sides, matching pairs.
Yet society eliminates 1/2 of the options when it comes
to defining and experiencing trust.
Society traditionally looks at & defines only the
positive side of trust.

LESSON 25 - TRUST: DILEMMA & CONFLICT

<u>trust: the dilemma</u>

You want to trust!

> When the traditional definition
> limits your choices to
> half of the realities,
> you're in a bind,
> faced with a
> dilemma.

Because you want to trust,
when someone clearly and consistently
lies to you,

> you ignore the negative reality &
> give them another chance by
> asking a question hoping
> that this time they will
> tell you the truth.

Then,
when
they
lie
to
you
again,
you
are
angry
with
them.

**Instead of ignoring
the negative reality
they have presented to you
time and time again,
face it
and tell yourself
that you trust
that they will lie to you.**

You then have the option to not ask the question.

trust: the conflict

Your best friend is always late.
She is also always very supportive.

When she learns you need a ride
to a very important meeting,
she assures you that
she will be on time.

A skunk doesn't change
what it is just because
it wants to no matter how
strong the motivation

REALITY
DOESN'T
CHANGE
LIKE
THAT.

**People
are
neither
good
or
bad.
They
are
made
up
of
both
positive
and
negative
behaviors.**

Instead of accepting her
offer of a ride,
trust that she'll be late.

That doesn't make
her a bad person.

Because she's
consistently supportive,
invite her over for coffee
later when the
time of her arrival
won't matter
and her support will.

LESSON 26 - TRUST: REDEFINED & LANGUAGE
trust: redefined

> **➤TRUST**
> **REALITY**
> **that is**
> **CLEAR,**
> **CONSISTENT,**
> **INTERNAL**
> **and**
> **NEUTRAL.**

Trust
is not
of or in
another
individual.

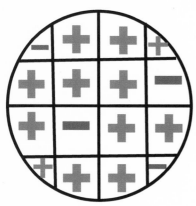

Trust is you
seeing
the many individual
behaviors
both
positive & negative
that combine to
make a person.

I trust my mother to be late.
A reality that has a negative value.
I trust mom to be creative.
A reality that has a positive value.

It creates choice.

It allows acceptance
of the individual's positives.

It allows rejection
of the individual's negatives
without rejecting
the individual.

the language of trust

Eliminate the words -
"I don't trust..."

Use instead

I trust him in a negative
way to
lie to me
about unimportant things.
(cap off the tooth paste)

I trust him in a
positive way to
provide the financial
support our family
needs.

When a
clear & consistent
reality
is presented,
trust
exists.

**Always
say what
you do
trust,
not
what
you
don't.
Saying
what
you
trust
(whether
positive
or
negative)
provides
you with
options.**

When a
new & different
clear & consistent
reality
is presented,
a new trust has
been established.

I use the rule of 3.
When a new clear
behavior is presented
3 times a
consistency exists

Trust changes as reality changes.

NOTES

3RD
SEASON

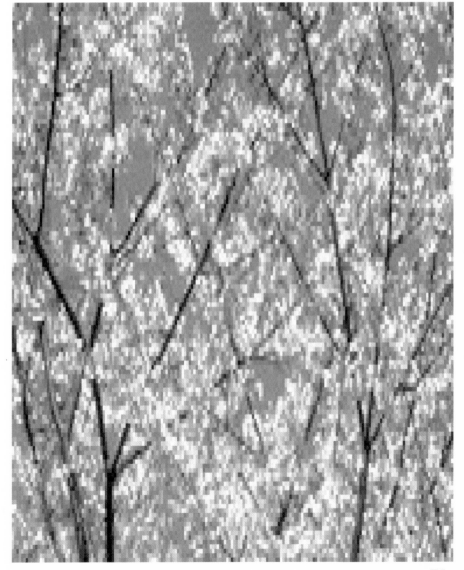

LESSON 27 - COMMUNICATION

In the beginning when caves were home,
the first communication was simple.

Someone saw something they wanted,
pointed and grunted.

If they were lucky they got a
      handful of the meat they wanted,
          not the turnips they didn't.

➤ **COMMUNICATION**
Convey or receive information.

That had it's
limitations.
They couldn't
talk about the
great hunt
of the
year before.

So
WALL ART
became
a new
form
of
communication.

That
served
fairly
well
until
people
became
mobile.
They
couldn't
take
walls
with
them.

It also didn't
help tell what
they wanted
for dinner the
next night.

Oral language
developed to
serve that need.

72

The head of the clan would pass down information about the best hunting sites from one generation to the next to the next.

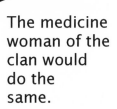

The medicine woman of the clan would do the same.

Along the chain, information would be lost in the telling or the remembering.

That problem was solved by the creation of writing as a form of communication.

Writing was initially an intricate, slow, art form.

It was not available to the masses.

The creation of the printing press made communication - the passing of information from one person to the next & from one generation to the next - available to anyone who wanted to be involved.

LESSON 28 - COMMUNICATION TYPES & FORMS

I. VERBAL COMMUNICATION

FORM A
The use of language in a spoken, oral form.

FORM B
The use of language in a written, non-oral form.

FORM C
The use of language using signs.

II. NONVERBAL COMMUNICATION

FORM A
The use of availability to communicate.

Your presence conveys caring.

When you verbally indicate availability but are not physically or emotionally available, your action speaks louder than words.

FORM B
The use of silence to communicate.

Silence allows you to listen and hear.

When you withhold information and remain silent as punishment your actions are deadly.

III. PHYSICAL COMMUNICATION

FORM A

The use of touch to communicate.

When you use the sense of touch as a means of conveying comfort, support, understanding or emotion you speak a language louder and more powerful than words.

It's unfortunate that the opposite is also true. Hitting & other forms of physical violence also communicates.

It is a scientifically proven fact that infants fail to grow and thrive when touch is withheld.

So grab someone to hug for their benefit and for yours.

FORM B Communication thru
facial expression & body language.

Studies have shown that facial expressions - happy, sad, surprise, anger - are universally recognized regardless of ethnic background, racial identity or language.

Even when you believe you are masking your feelings, they usually come through loudly and clearly.

75

LESSON 29 - VERBAL COMMUNICATION

> ➤**VERBAL COMMUNICATION**
> **The use of language,**
> **in oral, written or signed form**
> **to convey or receive information.**

➤Ambidextrous use of both hands with equal ease. Few people have this ability

➤Ambiverbal equal ease with the use of both oral & written language.

Few people have this ability.

COMMUNICATION OUTPUT [TEACHING]

You do not convey verbal information equally well in both an oral and a written form. Learn your dominant form and use it.

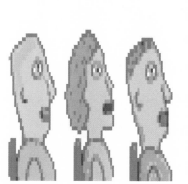

COMMUNICATION INTAKE [LEARNING]

You do not receive verbal information equally well in both an oral and a written form. Learn your dominate form and use it.

LESSON 30 - DOMINATE ABILITIES

COMMUNICATION
OUTPUT
[TEACHING]

When someone
asks you
for directions
to your home,
is it easier
to tell them
or to
write it out?

You'll have better
results when
you use your
dominant ability.

You try to tell
your daughter
how to do a
project but can't
get the thoughts
out clearly.
You're a
better writer
so write it down.

You also have to determine the dominate ability
of those people you interact with frequently.

 **Your boss provides info best
in an oral form.
Don't ask for a memo.
It will be garbled & unclear.
Ask her to tell you
while you write it down.**

COMMUNICATION INTAKE
[LEARNING]

When someone makes a
request of you is it easier to
remember after you
hear it or after reading it?

Determine the
dominate
intake ability
of those
people you
interact with
frequently.

You listen carefully
and still have trouble learning in a
class with a teacher who lectures
and doesn't give handouts.
You're not an oral learner.
Learn how to take excellent notes.

Again you'll have
better results
when you use
your dominant ability.

Your spouse seldom does the chores ✳
he agreed to do when you talked. ✳✳
It's probably not
personal or intentional.
Write a list and
give it to him when you talk.

LESSON 31 - POWER LANGUAGE

> ➤
> **POWER**
> **LANGUAGE**
>
> **Language**
> **that**
> **Is**
> **clear,**
> **definitive,**
> **effective,**
> **and**
> **efficient,**
> **&**
> **indicates**
> **choice**
> **and**
> **action.**

"I" STATEMENTS

Pick the most powerful word in communication.

More than one letter?
Not the best choice.

No matter how nice the tone,
when anyone says <u>you</u>
an automatic wall goes up
as people
automatically prepare
themselves for
what comes next.

Instead of
"you don't look good in that red dress"
use
✻✻"I like you better in your green dress".

"I" provides an opinion.

that allows others
to accept or reject
the information
without the need to defend.

POSITIVE REINFORCING LANGUAGE	INEFFECTUAL LANGUAGE for ELIMINATION
YES or NO ———————————— MAYBE	
WHEN ————————————————— IF	
AND ——————————————————— BUT	
WILL or WON'T —————————— CAN'T or TRY	
WANT TO ———————————————— SHOULDN'T	
I'LL FIND OUT ——————————— DON'T KNOW	
All indicate that you have made a decision; are taking charge.	All indicate you haven't made a decision or that you give the decision to others.

POWER LANGUAGE WORKSHEET

positive reinforcing language	my language for elimination

LESSON 32 - ORGANIC COMMUNICATION

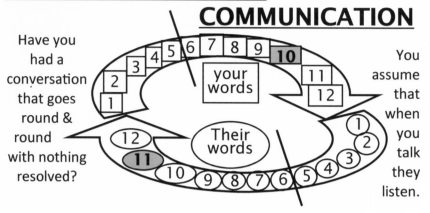

Have you had a conversation that goes round & round with nothing resolved?

You assume that when you talk they listen.

The reality is that when you talk, they listen to the first 5 or 6 words you say and then stop listening.

They use the rest of the time that you're talking to decide how they will answer.

Then you do the same to them.

You talk about what you think the is subject based on the 5 or 6 words.

The subject didn't come up until after words 10 & 11.

There is a solution.
ORGANIC COMMUNICATION

PURPOSE	REASON
action promotion	allows active listening keeps conversation on track
argument diffusion	maintain objectivity/equilibrium
fact finding	places responsibility appropriately
identification/ sorting	information/issues thoughts/feelings

➤ORGANIC COMMUNICATION™
A form of communication, utilizing five components, that enhances listening & the ability to respond appropriately.

ORGANIC COMMUNICATION™ COMPONENTS

1. use 5 words or less
2. repetition
3. action words, nouns, verbs
4. never justify;
5. answer only asked questions; statements are best, when asking a question use components 1 thru 4

METHOD

1. Organic Communication™
2. when appropriate switch to full conversation
3. return to Organic Communication™ if person disengages or argues
4. return to full conversation when equilibrium/movement is reestablished
5. throughout —

LISTEN
THEY WILL GIVE YOU YOUR CUES
STAY ON TASK

LESSON 33 - LIFE FOUNDATION:
DEFINITIONS

➤ORGANIC CHILD
A child in a natural, healthy state;
uncontaminated by adults;
usually nonexistent past the age of 6.

➤ORGANIC ADULT
An adult who has
reclaimed their
natural,
healthy state;
one who is
self nurturing;
LIVING,
not just existing.

➤ORGANIC PARENT
An adult who
nurtures his/her
charges & teaches
them how to be
healthy, thinking,
independent,
functioning
individuals.

➤TOYS/GAMES/PLAY
A child's job.
The way that a child learns how to:
relate, make decisions, set limits,
learn success and disappointment
and how to win and lose gracefully.

Adults must encourage children to play.

Adults must relearn how to enjoy play.

GLUE & FOUNDATION BUILDING BLOCKS

A house built without
a strong foundation,
will collapse.

No matter how you
shore it up,
paint it,
landscape,
or
decorate —
it will collapse.

Without a glue
the foundation,
No matter
how carefully laid,
will not remain intact.

**A
life
built
without
a
strong
foundation
will
also
collapse.**

LESSON 34 - THE GLUE: ACTION

ACTION

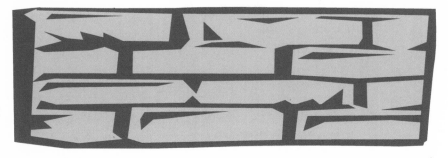

**is the mortar that holds the
five basic building blocks together.**

ACTION
TO DO.
to:

be	trust	bond	act
listen	hear	choose	decide
grow	change	receive	give
play	work	dream	plan
dance	sing	read	ask
tell	feel	go	stay

the organic child

Organic children act.

    She and he run, jump, climb and swim.
        They dance, skip, race, crawl, creep
            and twirl in circles big and small.

They sing, whistle, hum, yell, shout, and cry.

There are beds to jump on, leaves to jump in,
    stairs
        to bump
            down and
                to crawl up backwards.

    Children do and as they do
        they know
            they learn
                and understand.

Until —
    society tells them:
        to stop running and jumping
            because they will fall.

    society asks them why they sing and hum
        and tells them that the humming
        "is driving me crazy."

society says it's:
    dangerous to jump on the bed
        messy to ruin nicely raked leaves
            and silly to bump down stairs
                or to climb up backwards.

Action is the method that brings the blocks together and cements them into a strong foundation of extraordinary living.

Adults must become more childlike by embracing the actions of children.

LESSON 35 - FOUNDATION BLOCK 1: ESTEEM

Self esteem is the foundation block that anchors the other four basic foundation building blocks together.

> **➤SELF ESTEEM**
> **Specialness**
> **due to**
> **Existence.**

Self-Esteem
is not based
On what one does.

However -

What one does
is often
based
on
recognition
of one's
self-esteem

When one
recognizes their
own value -
One acts in a
positive way.

They treat
themselves kindly
and engage in joy-
ful activity.

They seek out
people who are
healthy.

When one fails to recognize their own value
they treat themselves with disdain.

They engage in activities and with people
who confirm their opinion of their low value.

Self-esteem
is the
cornerstone block
of the
Living Foundation
upon and around which
the other foundation block are placed.
Without it, life collapses.

CHAPTER 36 - FOUNDATION BLOCK 2: INSTINCT

> **➤INSTINCT**
> **Accumulated experience.**

Your

"gut reactions"

are based on

repeated
experiences

with reality.

They form your
instinct.

Without the ability to accept your gut reaction,
which is instinct,
life becomes a frightening series of
unpredictable events.

The ability to recognize your esteem
is closely tied
to your success in
developing you instinct.
The higher your esteem recognition,
the stronger your instinct.

Instinct is the
acceptance of the
reality that exists.

One doesn't have to like
the reality that exists.

One must accept that reality
before going on to
create a different reality.

Not wanting
to accept the reality
that
someone will
hurt you -
when
the reality is
that they have
hurt you
many times before -
will put you in
position to be
hurt again & again.

Only by
taking your head out of the sand
can you work to make that
unpleasant reality different.

CHAPTER 37 - FOUNDATION BLOCK 3: DECISION MAKING

> **➤DECISION MAKING**
>
> **The skill to make choices in a timely manner.**

It is a skill acquired thru practice.

You are not born with a finite number of decisions available to you.

An

infinite number

is available to you.

Picture this. You drive down a street that you've never been on before. The light turns yellow.

You play foot tag with the brake trying to decide if you have time to get thru the light before it turns red.

You finally put on the brake.

Another day.

A street you've driven many times before.
The light turns yellow.

You're by the Elm tree.

Your instinct kicks in
and you know that you
can safely make it thru
the light before it
turns red.

You are able to make the decision based
on accumulated experience, instinct.

Is it possible to learn to make the
RIGHT decision most of the time? **No!**

There is no such thing as a RIGHT decision.
The outcome of a decision can't be determined
until after it is made and acted upon.

Don't paralyze yourself trying
to make the RIGHT decision.

There are only decisions with
positive or negative outcomes.

With practice one develops skill in making decisions
with positive outcomes most of the time!

Positive outcomes require
that you continue to make decisions
by acting on instinct & information you possess.

93

LESSON 38 - FOUNDATION BLOCK 4: TRUST

> **➤TRUST**
> **reality**
> **that**
> **is**
> **clear,**
> **consistent,**
> **internal**
> **and**
> **neutral.**

The
building block
of
TRUST
tumbles down
when it is not
supported
by the blocks of
instinct
and
decision making
grounded in
esteem
and held fast by
action..

With
the

block
of
self-
esteem

When an adult
follows through
on a promise made,
a child learns to
believe in that
reality and trusts
the person in a
positive way
to do
what has been
promised.

block
of
instinct

block
of
decision
making

When an adult
repeatedly fails to
follow through on promises,
the child learns to
believe in that reality
and trusts the person in a
negative way to disappoint.

the
Reality
of
TRUST
is able to be
experienced.

From
experience
children learn to
trust the reality
presented to them
that when a parent
says "maybe"
it usually turns in to
"no".

**Children
experience
trust
in its
purest
form.
Adults
can
relearn
how to.**

95

LESSON 39 -
FOUNDATION BLOCK 5:
BONDING & RELATIONSHIP

> ➤**BONDING & RELATIONSHIP SKILLS**
> **Recognizing, developing and maintaining healthy relationships & the ability to form strong bonds.**

When you feel the worse and want most to avoid people —
is when you need people the most.

Seek out healthy relationships.

You need people in your life.

Relationships don't seek you.

When your esteem recognition is strong
you allow people to stay in your life.

With developed
instinct you don't
question
impressions that
you experience
meeting someone.

With sound
decision making ability
you don't
second guess
your instincts
or allow
important decisions
to be made for you
by default.

A healthful
trust perspective
allows you to create
an environment
that is
safe and secure.

If this very old joke applies to you —

'Any club that would have me as a member I wouldn't want to belong to'—

your relationship and bonding skills need improvement, starting with esteem and moving on thru instinct, decision making and trust.

NOTES

4TH
SEASON

LESSON 40 -
ORGANIC GROWTH EXERCISES (OGe™)

Now that you know what the
basic building blocks are,
you may ask, "How do I get
them?" First —

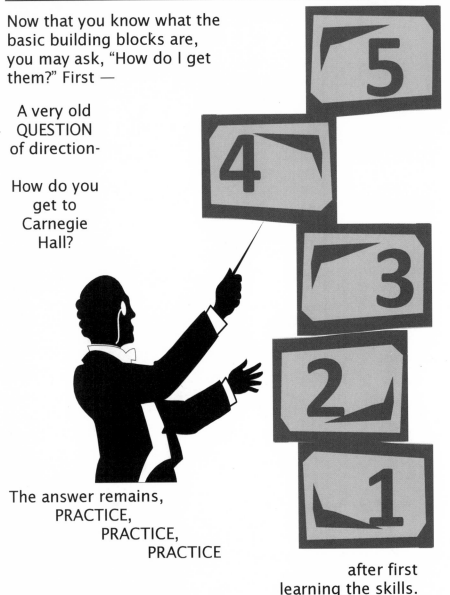

A very old
QUESTION
of direction-

How do you
get to
Carnegie
Hall?

The answer remains,
PRACTICE,
PRACTICE,
PRACTICE

after first
learning the skills.

Life is a series of habits.
Some good habits and some bad.
The skills of life are acquired, healthy habits.
Living well is the habit of using those skills.

The
answer
is also
the same
when you
ask other
questions-

How do I become healthy?
PRACTICE, PRACTICE, PRACTICE

What do I have to do?
Select the skills you need.

Is it complicated?
It's simple. Few things are complicated.

Is it hard?
It's work. It is neither easy or hard.

How do I maintain my health once I develop it?
**By remembering the foundations and
practicing the skills of living on a daily basis.**

What are the foundation skills I need to learn?

>ORGANIC GROWTH EXERCISES™
**The five organic exercises
that promote health & well-being.**

**Do Something Good (DSG) for yourself
Do Something Fun (DSF) that a kid under 7 would do
Do a Coloring Book (DCB)
Do Something Wacky (DSW)
Do Something Courageous (DSC)**

Check the details in the pages that follow.

LESSON 41 - DO SOMETHING GOOD

> **➤DOING SOMETHING GOOD**
> **(for self)**
> **doing something**
> **that treats you nicely**
> **with you as the primary beneficiary.**

DON'T
WAIT
until
you
feel
you
deserve
it.

DON'T
WAIT
until
you
feel
good
about
yourself.

DON'T
wait on
or
depend on
someone else
to do for you
what
you
must
do for yourself.

✳︎
✳︎✳︎
DO IT
until
you
know
that
you
deserved
it
all
along!

**Too many people wait
until they feel good
about themselves
before they do
good things
for themselves.**

**It doesn't happen
that way.**

**Reverse the process.
Do good
till it feels good.**

When you decide
to go to lunch
with a friend
because you
enjoy their
company,
you are
Doing
Something
Good
(**DSG**)
for yourself.

If you do it
because you
owe her for something
she did for you,
it doesn't fit as a
DSG.

**DO
SOMETHING
GOOD
FOR
YOURSELF
AT
LEAST
ONCE
EVERY
OTHER
WEEK.**

LESSON 42 - DO SOMETHING FUN

> **➤DOING SOMETHING FUN**
> **(that a kid under 7 would do)**
> **Activities done just for the fun of it.**
> **A way to relieve pressure of everyday living.**

ADULT SKIING

Adults attach
a purpose
to their fun.
They want to
get the most value
from their lift tickets,
to develop their skills,
to get a good workout
and want to have their
clothes
color coordinated.

KID SKIING

They just want
to have fun.
They don't care about
value,
they don't care if they
fall down,
what clothes they wear
or whether they are
getting a good workout.

DSF   DO
SOMETHING
        FUN

❄️
**Do
Something
Fun
at
least
once
every
other
week.**

**Alternate
with
Do
Something
Good
DSG.**

LESSON 43 - DO COLORING BOOK

➤DO A COLORING BOOK
The selection, purchase
and use of a coloring
book & crayons as tools
in the development of
healthy, basic skills.

Do you hate
to color?

If so,
search your
memory and
you will find
an incident
that ruined
for you
a wonderful
process.

Someone wrongly told you:
"stay inside the lines"
        or "
the sky isn't orange,
it should to be blue."

Coloring
is one of the
most important
tools in a child's
(or adult's)
growth process.

It teaches and helps
the individual develop
5
specific & important skills.

✱
✱✱ Go buy yourself a coloring book & crayons
& experience the joy & growth for yourself.

DEVELOPS INSTINCT
Looking over all the books
available allows you to get in
touch with your likes and dislikes.
You learn to follow your instincts.

DEVELOPS DECISION MAKING ABILITY
The choice of the book, the page,
the color in each section on the page
all help develop decision making.
You color the ocean red,
decide you don't like it.
Next time you use purple.
You've learned that you can keep
making decisions til you get
it the way YOU want it to be.

AWARD / REWARD
You need a quick pick me up.
Putting together a model or knitting takes time.
Coloring a page can take as little as 15 minutes.

PROBLEM SOLVING TOOL
When your
conscious mind is
occupied with coloring
your sub-conscious
is able to
identify the problem
that your
conscious mind can't.
It may even be able
to find a solution.

RELEASE
Coloring
can help you
identify and
release the
emotions
- anger, sadness,
disappointment -
that are causing
you distress.

LESSON 44 - DO SOMETHING WACKY

Did
you
ever
watch a child
bump
down the steps
on their bottom
then get up
&
walk away
laughing?

They
know
how
to
relieve,
momentarily,
the strain
of
living life.

> ➤WACKY
> **something without**
> **purpose or process;**
> **no beginning,**
> **middle or end;**
> **done just because;**
> **legal**
> **and**
> **nondangerous.**

Life can
be a
pressure
cooker
and
when we
don't vent
the steam,
we blow.

Most of the things that
we do in life
require planning & process.

Sometimes we just need to do something
that has no meaning,
        is not a process
                & is not planned.

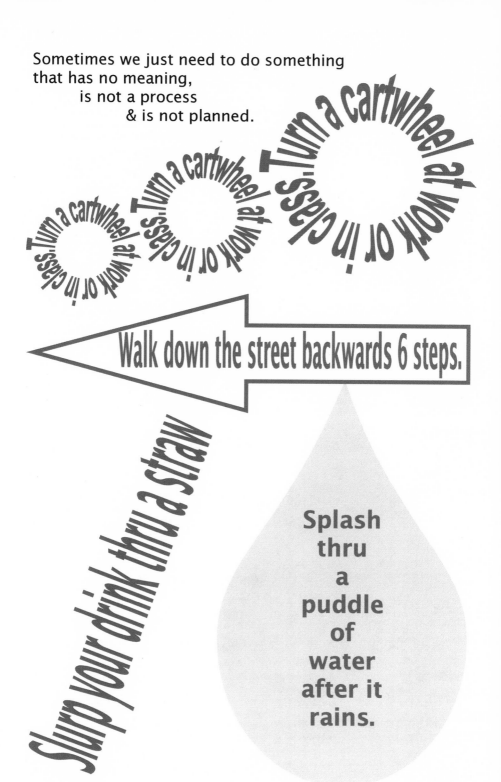

Turn a cartwheel at work or in class.

Walk down the street backwards 6 steps.

Slurp your drink thru a straw

Splash
thru
a
puddle
of
water
after it
rains.

LESSON 45 - DO SOMETHING COURAGEOUS

➤**COURAGE**
being afraid
and
going ahead
anyway;
not
the absence
of fear.

It is not necessary
to overcome
every fear.

Overcome
only those fears
that are holding
you back & are
preventing you
from doing what
you want to do.

You live
on the
north
Atlantic
coast
and
fear
flying.

Your ideal vacation is
sailing and swimming.

You'll never vacation in the Hawaii

but you don't care.

There's no need to overcome your fear of flying.

A promotion you want
requires you to fly to
California monthly.

Your fear is
holding you hostage.
Find the way to do it
even while you
remain afraid.

Define fear as the
positive tool that it is.

Embrace fear as a
protective device.

A chosen
act of
courage
is to be
done no
more than
twice in
12
months.

Find a way to
move past
your fear.

That is the
act of courage.

REMEMBER -
Too many people
define fear
in negative terms
as unknown,
uncontrollable;
a weakness.

And that
none of the words
used to describe fear
is pleasant.

➤FEAR
a
reasonable
response
to
a
real
or
perceived
danger.

Good reason
that no one
wants to experience
or admit to fear.

LESSON 46 -
CREATED FAMILY VILLAGE™

You need someone to fill each of 8 essential roles.

➤**CREATED FAMILY VILLAGE™**
**Persons who fulfill any of
the eight essential roles that provide
support, encouragement and understanding
making life more complete.**

Have no
one person fill more than
3
of the essential roles.

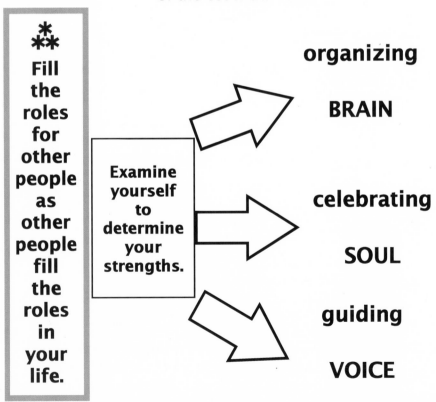

**✳✳✳
Fill
the
roles
for
other
people
as
other
people
fill
the
roles
in
your
life.**

**Examine
yourself
to
determine
your
strengths.**

organizing

BRAIN

celebrating

SOUL

guiding

VOICE

CREATED FAMILY VILLAGE™ - worksheets

You'll have a minimum of 3 people that you trust
in a positive way supporting you and your efforts.

CREATED FAMILY VILLAGE™ - RECEIVING

Person(s) who is(are) your voice		
Person(s) who is(are) your sight		
Person(s) who is(are) your heart		
Person(s) who is(are) your soul		
Person(s) who is(are) your brain		
Person(s) who is(are) your body		
Person(s) who is(are) your imagination		
Person(s) who is your memory		

HOW I WILL SEARCH OUT PEOPLE TO FILL ROLES	ROLES THAT ARE MY STRENGTHS AND WHY THEY ARE	

CREATED FAMILY VILLAGE™ - GIVING

Person(s) for whom I am voice		
Person(s) for whom I am sight		
Person(s) for whom I am heart		
Person(s) for whom I am soul		
Person(s) for whom I am brain		
Person(s) for whom I am body		
Person(s) for whom I am imagination		
Person(s) for whom I am memory		

 **Limit the roles you provide to 3.
Avoid over-taxing yourself.**

VOICE

> **mentor or guide**
> **The one with whom you**
> **mull over decisions,**
> **whose insight you trust.**

At times we need someone who will guide us
along the path toward a decision.

A person who provides us with a voice
saying the things we censor ourselves from saying.

A person who says the things
that we need to hear even when
It is something we don't want to hear.
or tells us to do the things we want to put off.

It is the person who mentors us.

We say to them:

" I'd like your
feedback on a
decision about
my job."

**And they give
us a voice
outside
ourselves to
reflect on.**

LESSON 47 - VOICE: MIRROR/SEER

SIGHT

> ➤
> **mirror or seer**
> **One who listens to your**
> **intrinsic self,**
> **through whom**
> **you reveal you to yourself.**

One doesn't always need to hear
another's opinion.

What one needs to know is
already a part of our being.

What is needed
is to have our own thoughts
reflected back to us.

Someone who acts as a mirror.

**They are able to
quietly listen while
we cleanse ourselves
of our doubts allowing
us to move forward.**

" Thanks for
listening,
I didn't know
I felt that
deeply."

LESSON 48 - HEART:
HEALER/WITCH-DOCTOR

HEART

> ➤
> **healer or witch-doctor**
> **The one who helps you reconnect,**
> **who reminds you that**
> **you are important enough**
> **to take care of yourself.**

Society teaches us to look out for others
often at the expense of ourselves.

We need then, someone to look out for us.
Someone to see what we overlook.
Someone who can override our hesitancy
to take care of ourselves.

Sometimes it is the body they help heal.
Sometimes it is the spirit or the heart.

Sometimes they help us heal
from the slings and arrows that wound us
in the course of daily living.

" What you need is a
good hot bowl of chicken soup.
Climb in bed and I'll bring it to you."

SOUL

> **ritualizer**
> **or**
> **ceremony-maker**
> **The one who makes place or moment significant.**

Ceremony and ritual signify
change & constancy.

The engagement party = new love.
The wedding ceremony = commitment
The christening = new life
School graduation = adulthood
Funeral service = loss & remembrance

Birthdays, holidays, promotions & retirements
provide a time for togetherness & reward.

Someone must make sure that we mark
all the moments in our lives
for lasting joy and for remembrance.

**" Come on over for tea.
I'll get out my best china."**

**"A baby?!"
I'll plan a shower."**

LESSON 49 - BRAIN:
STRUCTURER/ORDER-BRINGER

BRAIN

> ➤
> **structurer**
> **or**
> **order-bringer**
> **The one who helps you find self-discipline and order.**

If we could do it for ourselves there wouldn't
be a booming market for:
self-help books & video tapes on exercise
weight loss & exercise groups
personal trainers
time management experts
closet organizers.

I call them professional nags.
And I mean that in the nicest of ways.
We need someone outside ourselves
to help us develop the healthy habits
we want and don't yet have.

**" Why don't you join an exercise group
or get a personal trainer?"**

LESSON 49 - BODY:
COMPANION/JOURNEY-SHARER

BODY

> ➤
> **companion**
> **or**
> **journey-sharer**
> **The one**
> **with whom**
> **you create**
> **adventure,**
> **pleasure**
> **and**
> **excitement.**

Solitude is wonderful on occasion.

Other times require someone to share
the adventure, pleasure & excitement.

At times someone else
(a child, a grandchild, a spouse or niece)
is the reason we create the journey.

Sometimes it takes another person
to create for us
what we are not able or willing
to create for ourselves.

" Let's do a train trip cross county this summer."

LESSON 50 - IMAGINATION: MAGICIAN/PERMISSION GIVER

IMAGINATION

> **magician**
> **or**
> **permission-giver**
> **The one who opens up possibility by encouraging you to try new or different things.**

We become so set in our ways that we
can't see the trees for the forest.

We spend our time dong the things that
we have to do - work the job to pay bills.

Our talents and interests lay forgotten for
the odd moments we spare to indulge.

We are too critical of ourselves in ways
that we would never be critical of others.

Our magician waves the magic wand and says -
"Go for it."

**" Have you ever thought about painting
as a business, not just as a hobby?"**

LESSON 50 - MEMORY:
STORY-TELLER/ELDER

MEMORY

**story-teller
or
elder
The one
who
connects
you
to tradition
and/or
personal
history.**

The present is important as one
works toward ones future.

A connection with the past is important as a guidepost.

Being reminded of the good times
when times aren't so good.

Being reminded of how far we have come
when we feel we haven't gone anywhere.

**" Mom, remember
when we went
camping and..."**

**" I remember a time
when your mother
dated your dad and..."**

LESSON 51 - TEAMS

> ➤TEAMS
> **People who work together
> for a common goal.**

TEAM MAY FALL INTO THE CATEGORIES OF:
  Family   Workforce   Organizations
          Committee   Board
              Spiritual Community

SUCCESS FORMULA $S = (CV)^4 + T$

Common Goal/Vision   + Timetable
(dream & measurable objective)

Complexity/View   (varied skills & accountability)

Credibility/Value   (skill level & abilities)

Commitment/Vigor (energy & synergy)

TEAM TYPES	PURPOSE	FRAMEWORK
Seed Developmental	Create	Start & Stop date
Root Peer/Level	Support Information	Ongoing Never ending
Garden Growth	Production Expansion	Varies

122

TEAM DYNAMICS	
5 TEAM STAGES	**PURPOSE & BEHAVIOR**
FORMING	**Reason for getting together** Vision determined Norms defined Roles created & assigned
STORMING	**Processing and Reforming** Confusion Triangulation & Undermining Stab the Leader & Backbiting
NORMING	**Productivity & Synergy begin** People rise to the occasion People take on responsibility Feeling of family begins
PERFORMING	**++ Productivity** People rise above the norm People become self-directed Business/Meetings are smooth
CELEBRATING	**Key to ongoing productivity** Recreating Honoring Rewarding

Teams are essential whether family or business.
Teams are integral structures
when working for a successful outcome.
Determine you needs & develop them effectively.

AN IMPORTANT NOTE
When teams fail to celebrate they begin to fail.
Monetary rewards, awards & certificates are not enough.
Those that party together, produce to the max.

LESSON 52:
VISION, LIVING GOALS™ & SUCCESS

>**VISION**
Dream
+
Measurable
Objective.

❀❀**VISIONING**
1. Quantify dream.
2. Determine needs & want.
3. Set objectives.
4. Secure support.
5. Follow-up with action.

Objectives are
desire & means
to reach a
goal!

>**GOALS**
Vision
+
Timetable.

❀❀**GOAL PLANNING**
1. Verify vision, needs & wants.
2. Chart route.
3. Set goals.
4. Secure & use support.
5. Follow-thru with actions.

Goals are made up of specific objectives.
"I'm going to spend some time
being good to myself" won't cut it.
"I'm going to read a book & take 2 bubble baths
[measurable - you do it or you don't]
each week for the next 6 months [timetable].

GOALS CLUB

✸Join the 430 club
Don't just plan 1 or 2 goals a year.
You deserve constant reward for hard work.

365 daily goals/no matter how small
                may or may not relate to
                weekly, monthly or annual
52 weekly goals/a bit bigger than daily ones
                may or may not relate to
                monthly or annual goals
12 monthly goals/bigger still
                may or may not relate to annual goal
1 annual goal/may or may not relate
                to a long term (5 year) plan

1 goal completed.
You've read this book
& begun to establish healthy new habits.

CONGRATULATIONS

➤SUCCESS is doing!
the only failure
is not trying.

MY CONCLUDING THOUGHTS

I hope that much of what you have read
touches a place deep within you.
A place that is saying to you
"I knew there was something more!"

That is your healthy child waiting
to be reawakened, waiting to live
the extraordinary life it was born to live.

We desire better than we have been led to believe.
Happiness, joy, excitement, creativity &
self-appreciation are there for our taking.

I hope reading this page is not your conclusion.
Reading this book is only a beginning.
The work now begins.

Go back to the chapters and methodically work on
making the definitions, concepts, strategies, skills &
tools an active expression of your everyday being.
Make them your habit.

There is also available a
workbook of forms to help you form your habits.

Be in touch.
Together we will do extraordinary things.
Marta

The purchase of this book entitles you to up to
5 emails with Marta.
action@trainingwithmarta.com